An Educator's Guide to
Differentiating Instruction

HOUGHTON MIFFLIN **GUIDE SERIES**

An Educator's Guide to
Differentiating Instruction

Carol Ann Tomlinson
University of Virginia

James M. Cooper, Series Editor
University of Virginia

HOUGHTON MIFFLIN COMPANY   BOSTON   NEW YORK

KH

Senior Sponsoring Editor: Sue Pulvermacher-Alt
Senior Development Editor: Lisa Mafrici
Editorial Assistant: Dayna Pell
Manufacturing Coordinator: Chuck Dutton
Marketing Manager: Jane Potter

Printed in the U.S.A.

ISBN: 0-618-57283-X

6789-VHO-09 08

11/2/09

CONTENTS

Preface   vii

Part I: Introduction   1

Part II: Knowledge   5

    The Classroom as a System   5

    Understanding Who We Teach   5

    Understanding Where We Teach   11

    Understanding What We Teach   13

    Understanding How We Teach   15

    Key Principles of Effective Differentiation   16

    Removing Barriers to Effective Differentiation   20

    The Importance of Intent and Persistence   24

Part III: Applications   26

    Early Steps in Differentiation   26

    Curriculum 1st—Then Pre-Assessment   26

    Develop a Mental Image of Your Classroom   28

    Become a Student of Your Students   28

    Plan for Success   29

    Talk with Your Students about Differentiation   31

    Think about "Ranges"   31

    Think Information, Not Grade Book   33

    Options for Early Differentiation   33

Part IV: Extensions   36

For Reflection   41

Glossary   43

References   46

PREFACE

Houghton Mifflin Company publishes outstanding education textbooks in the areas of foundations of education, introduction to education, educational psychology special education, and early childhood education. These textbooks introduce students to many concepts, policies, and research that undergird educational practice. However, as is the case for virtually all introductory texts, many topics are introduced but not covered in great depth. The Houghton Mifflin Teacher Education Guide Series is designed to provide more in-depth coverage of selected educational topics studied in the teacher education curriculum.

At the present time, there are ten guides in the series:

- Classroom Management

- Field-Based Classroom Observation

- Diversity in the Classroom

- Classroom Assessment

- Inclusion

- Technology Tools

- School-based Intervention Programs

- Student Motivation

- Teacher Reflection

- Differentiating Instruction

The topics for these guides were selected because they are addressed in virtually all teacher education programs, and contain vital information for beginning teachers if they are to be successful in the classroom. Instructors may use the guides either for required or enrichment reading.

Each of these guides provides pre-service teachers with greater in-depth knowledge, application suggestions, and additional resources on its particular topic. All the guides share a common format that includes an introduction to the topic, knowledge that the prospective teacher should possess about the topic, examples of and suggestions for how the knowledge can be applied, and resources for further exploration. Each guide also contains 10-15 questions designed to help the prospective teacher reflect on the concepts and ideas introduced in the guide, as well as a glossary of key terms.

Most teachers know that differentiating instruction for academically diverse students makes sense, but actually doing it in their classrooms is often difficult. In this guide, Carol Ann Tomlinson provides key principles for differentiating instruction, and ways by which to begin the process. She recognizes that differentiating instruction requires a commitment on the teacher's part, but that the know-how to implement differentiation develops over time. Tomlinson provides the beginning teacher with practical ways to begin this process.

An Educator's Guide to
Differentiating Instruction

PART I: INTRODUCTION

TEACHING IN ACADEMICALLY DIVERSE CLASSROOMS

When the school year begins, Ms. Alexander has mapped out the goals toward which she will guide her students over the course of their time with her. She has made sure her plans carefully reflect required standards and has crafted her plans with an eye to making learning both meaningful and engaging for her students. Her advance work with curriculum reflects her current best understanding of the content she will teach and her belief that an effective teacher continues to hone and polish curriculum plans.

As Ms. Alexander enters her classroom on the first day of school with her carefully developed lesson plans, a second key element in the teaching/learning process will soon appear. She will shortly meet a room full of students.

- Four of them are highly advanced academically for their grade and age. Three of the four are also emotionally and socially mature for their age. One is socially and emotionally less mature than most other students in the class.

- A number of the students have gaps in knowledge or skill that will prove problematic at one time or another as the year progresses. Six students in the class have at least some difficulty with reading and many are less than proficient in reading text material.

- Two students have identified learning disabilities.

- Three have problems with attention and hyperactivity.

- Two students are relatively new to the English language and two others have been speaking English for less than three years. At least six students in the class are from cultures different from the teacher's culture.

- Four students are having problems at home and come to school angry or afraid.

- Some of the students are very extraverted and love the opportunity to answer questions and engage in dialogue with the teacher and their peers. Some of the students are quiet and would prefer to recede into the background of the classroom landscape whenever possible.

- Some of the students tend to learn best when they hear explanations, some when they see demonstrations, some when they can read information.

Ms. Alexander has a choice to make when her lesson plans and the students intersect in the classroom. She can assume that as long as she covers the curriculum she has prepared, she is doing her job. Outcomes for students will vary—but that's to be expected. Or, she can decide that it is her job to study her students as well as her content and make modifications when advisable to ensure that each student has the best opportunity she can give that student to succeed as fully as possible in achieving designated goals—and in their development as learners.

Differentiating Instruction

Differentiated instruction is a way of thinking about teaching and learning. It works from the following assumptions:

- Students differ in their readiness to learn, in particular interests, and in how they learn.

- Student variance makes a difference in the learning process.

- Learning must happen within students, not "to" them.

- It is the teacher's job to teach students as well as content.

- Each student needs and deserves a teacher who will be an active partner in helping that student identify and build upon personal strengths, identify and address areas of weakness, and develop a sense of self-efficacy that comes from accomplishing important goals.

- The most effective teachers use assessment information to develop and modify instructional plans so that the classroom "works" for the various students in it.

- Classrooms that are effective for academically diverse populations define "fairness" as making sure everyone gets what he or she needs to succeed—not as treating everyone exactly alike.

Part of Successful Teaching

Teaching is about ensuring learning. Successful teachers do what it takes to make sure that each student has the best possible opportunity for success. For some students, success will mean moving well beyond grade-level goals. For some, it will mean becoming proficient with grade-level goals. For some, it will mean a journey "backwards" to fill gaps in precursor knowledge, understanding, and skill even as they move forward to work with new knowledge, understanding, and skill. For some students—for example, those who work with Individual Educational Plans designed to address severe learning challenges—success will be making small steps in the direction of fundamental competencies.

The most successful teachers work with the premise that their own success should be measured not by coverage of curriculum—but by the success of their students' learning. In its truest sense, teaching is not finished until learning occurs—for each learner. Teaching without learning is an oxymoron.

Successful teachers then, develop the best possible curriculum plans they can develop. They also develop instructional plans aimed at successful learning for each student. They use a continual stream of assessment data—both formal and informal—to help them understand where each student is in the learning journey at a given time and to guide adaptation of subsequent instruction so that students are learning as much as they can as efficiently as they can.

Differentiation, then, is a part of instruction. It is informed by assessment. It is in service of student success with curricular goals despite inevitable variance as learners.

A Closer Look	*The Teacher in Action*

As the year begins, Ms. Alexander prepares to pre-assess her students to determine their general proficiency with fundamental skills like reading and writing. She will survey them to begin learning about their interests and learning preferences. She will talk with them about their various strengths and needs and will begin involving them in describing the kind of classroom that would work best for them as individuals and for the class as a whole.

As the year goes on, she will continue to use her strong curriculum plans as a compass for her work and that of her students. She will also work consistently to develop flexibility in how she teachers and how her students learn in order to contribute to maximum growth for each learner. Among her goals will be flexible use of classroom space, student groupings, materials, her own mode of presentation, and ways students develop and display competencies.

A primary goal for Ms. Alexander as the year begins is establishing routines that will enlist her students as partners in making the classroom and its routines support the flexibility she needs in order to teach each student effectively.

PART II: KNOWLEDGE

THE CLASSROOM AS A SYSTEM

It's easy as teachers to focus so intently on "covering the curriculum" that we fail to take into account multiple elements in a classroom that work in an interdependent way. Thinking about those elements and how they interrelate provides a sound foundation for understanding and implementing what we call "differentiated instruction."

One way to envision the elements in the classroom system is to think about who we teach, where we teach, what we teach, and how we teach. Those four elements are highly dependent on one another, and in dynamic classrooms, the teacher not only takes into account and plans for the four elements separately, but also seeks a growing understanding of how each of the elements will shape the others.

Looking at the four elements also helps shape a rationale for differentiation.

Understanding Who We Teach

Human beings are shaped by many factors in their lives. Among those are: age, health, past experience, ability, gender, culture, race, neurological "wiring," interest, adult support, and peer interactions—to name a few. Sometimes these elements overlap, but each of them can play a potent role in how a student learns—and how that student views learning—at a given time and in a particular context.

In schools, we've attempted to "control for" one of the factors—age. We've done that by placing students of a similar chronological age in classrooms with age-mates. While that may have some merit, age-based grouping likely has had two negative outcomes. First, it has given us permission to believe that students of a similar age are essentially alike as learners. Second, it has caused us to underestimate and under attend to the impact of all the other factors on learning.

As educators, we have a great deal of theoretical, observational, and research-based knowledge about how learners are shaped by various factors in their lives. In fact, there may be so much information available about learner variance that it becomes overwhelming and paralyzing. To help with organizing the available information, it may be useful to think about learner differences in three broad categories—differences in readiness, interest, and learning profile. These are categories with direct applicability to instruction.

Considering Student Readiness Level

Readiness refers to a student's proximity to a particular learning goal or task. Readiness can be shaped by past experiences, personal strengths and weaknesses, learner self-confidence, and so on. It is also the case that readiness will fluctuate for a given student though a subject, across subjects, and in various classroom and non-school contexts.

Readiness is *not* a synonym for academic ability. It is possible for a student with high ability to struggle with a subject or a topic within a subject. It is also possible for a student with less academic ability to be quite strong with some areas of the curriculum. Further, we tend to think about ability as fixed. While it is actually the case that ability is malleable and can be significantly influenced for better or worse by environment, opportunity, and support, our perception about the fixedness of ability makes it important to veer away from persistent attention to what we perceive to be a student's ability level and to look more closely at where the student is in regard to current knowledge, understanding, skill, and classroom working conditions.

Many years of research on readiness and learning yield at least two key principles. First, when tasks are too hard or too easy for a student, significant learning will not likely occur. Second, for a student to learn robustly, required tasks and goals need to be a little in advance of the student's comfort level—and there needs to be a support system enabling the student to "extend his or her reach" to the new level of competence necessitated by the task. Thus learning evolves most appropriately when a student progressively encounters work that is just a little too hard for him or her, and when scaffolding that makes it possible for the student to achieve at the new level of expectations (Vygotsky, 1986; Bransford, Brown, & Cocking, 2000; Wolfe, 2001).

Practical Tips & Strategies	*Responding to Variance in Student Readiness*

To address variance in student readiness, teachers may use materials at different reading levels, meet with students in small groups for targeted instruction, assign homework matched to learner need, tier assignments, provide reading support for difficult materials, give advanced readers materials that are beyond grade level, assign spelling lists to individuals at their current level of skill, provide tape recordings of complex print material, provide graphic organizers to support note-taking, add student-specific goals to checklists for success, and so on. There are many ways to address a range of readiness needs even when all students are working toward common goals. In fact, it may be most important to attend to readiness when students work toward the same goals. In most classrooms, whatever the learning goal, it is likely to be too demanding for some students and too easy for others unless the teacher addresses readiness differences in some way(s).

Considering Student Interests

As human beings, we tend to find interesting those things that help us find meaning in our world and a sense of significance and purpose in our lives. When students are interested in what they are learning, the act of learning is satisfying. In such instances, students are engaged and ready to meet the challenges inherent in learning (Ginsberg & Wlodkowski, 2000).

Once again, we understand from theory, observation, and research, roles that student interest can play in learning. We know, for example, that interest and motivation are closely linked. That is, when what a student learns is a match for what the student cares about, it's likely that the student's motivation to learn will be increased. When motivation to learn increases, student outcomes are likely to be more favorable. In fact, research indicates that student attitude, persistence, and achievement improve when a student finds the work he or she does to be interesting (Tomlinson, et al., 2004).

Teachers can plan to enlist student interest in learning in two ways. First, it is possible and important to show students how the subjects we teach connect with their particular interests. Second, a wise teacher works persistently to help a student discover new interests by ensuring that what the student encounters in the classroom is engaging and satisfying. To assume we don't have time to address student interest is to assume we don't have time to tap their motivation to learn. Such decisions are likely to be expensive in terms of both short and long term outcomes.

Practical Tips & Strategies	*Responding to Variance in Student Interests*

There are many ways of addressing learner interests in the classroom. Among those are connecting content with students' cultures, experiences, and talents; showing students the usefulness of what they are learning in the lives of meaningful adults; showing students how concepts apply in domains beyond the one on which a lesson or unit focuses; using interest centers, interest groups, specialty groups, or expert groups; using simulations, problem-based learning, and other inquiry-oriented strategies, teaching with metaphors; encouraging students to select applications for the skills and understandings they are learning; using Jigsaw groups; and encouraging students to select free reading materials of interest to them.

Considering Student Learning Profile

Learning profile is a synonym for learning preference. As readiness is necessary for student growth and interest is necessary for motivation to learn, tapping a student's learning preference is necessary for efficiency of learning. Most of us can learn things in more than one way. It's also the case, however, that for most of us, some ways of learning will be a better "fit' for us than others.

Learning profile is shaped by at least four often-overlapping factors: learning style, gender, culture, and intelligence preference.

Learning style refers to environmental or contextual factors that can affect learning. For example, some students learn better in the presence of some sound or noise and some learn better in quiet. Some students need to sit at a desk or in a chair to read. Others are better readers when they can stretch out as they read. Some students learn more readily when then hear an explanation while others learn better by "doing," by reading, or through demonstration.

Gender also appears to shape learning patterns. In other words, there appear to be female-preferred approaches to learning (such as collaboration and discussion) and male-preferred approaches to learning (for example, competition and moving about while learning). While gender-related patterns of learning likely exist, it is not the case that all boys learn in the male-pattern mode or that all girls learn in the female-pattern mode (Gurian, 2001).

There also appear to be patterns of learning associated with particular cultures or groups of cultures. For example, members of some cultures show preference for task orientation to learning, while members of others seem to prefer a social orientation to learning. Some cultures tend to value group success over individual success, while members of other cultures tend to have the reverse inclination. Some cultures gravitate toward learning about concrete realities while others tend toward an interest in abstractions and ideas. Again, however, it will *not* be the case that all learners from a particular culture learn best in the same way (Lasley & Matczynski, 1997). To assume such similarity is to misunderstand the complexity that is inevitable in any group of people.

Finally, learning inclinations are affected by what some psychologists refer to as "intelligence preference." Intelligence preferences are shaped by neurological "wiring" and likely by other factors such as culture as well. Theorists and researchers have conceived intelligence preference somewhat differently. For example, Howard Gardner (1993) proposes at least eight neurologically-influenced ways of taking in or processing information. Robert Sternberg (1988) proposes three (analytical, practical, and creative approaches). Both remind us that (a) all people learn and work in multiple ways, (b) despite patterns that may exist within groups of people, no group is homogeneous and we should not generalize patterns to all individuals within a group, and (c) it is important for teachers to develop student strengths and help them compensate for weaknesses in the various intelligence areas.

There is research indicating positive impacts of addressing student preferences in learning style, culture, gender, and intelligence preference in the classroom across grades and subject areas (Tomlinson, et al., 2004).

Practical Tips & Strategies	Responding to Variance in Student Learning Profile

As is the case with readiness and interest, there are many ways of teaching in response to student learning profile needs. Among those are: making teacher presentations in multiple modalities, showing part to whole and whole to part relationships, allowing students to explore work and express what they have learned through a choice of modes, teaching and designing tasks with varied intelligence strengths and needs in mind, creating assessments that respond to different learning modes, allowing students to work alone or with peers, and teaching in culturally sensitive ways.

While readiness, interest, and learning profile differences do not encompass all learner variance, it is likely that teachers who persistently work to understand and address learner needs in these areas will develop classrooms that enable greater success for more students than had they not done so. It is also likely that because such teachers actively intend to know their students as individuals, these teachers will also come to understand other areas of student need, which they can address in flexible classroom settings.

Learning is not the only beneficiary of responsive instruction. Teaching itself is likely to become far more satisfying when teachers actively engage with the richness in the young lives they teach, as well as with the content they teach.

Practical Tips & Strategies	Addressing Student Learning Preferences

As the year begins, Ms. Alexander prepares to pre-assess her students to determine their general proficiency with fundamental skills like reading and writing. She will survey them to begin learning about their interests and learning preferences. She will talk with them about their various strengths and needs and will begin involving them in describing the kind of classroom that would work best for them as individuals and for the class as a whole.

As the year goes on, she will continue to use her strong curriculum plans as a compass for her work and that of her students. She will also work consistently to develop flexibility in how she teachers and how her students learn in order to contribute to maximum growth for each learner. Among her goals will be flexible use of classroom space, student groupings, materials, her own mode of presentation, and ways students develop and display competencies.

A primary goal for Ms. Alexander as the year begins is establishing routines that will enlist her students as partners in making the classroom and its routines support the flexibility she needs in order to teach each student effectively.

Understanding Where We Teach

Whether by intent or default, each teacher is a leader in developing a classroom environment that will impact student learning in a multitude of ways. In fact, the nature of the learning environment is a predictor of success or failure for diverse learning populations.

Few students bolt into classrooms each year—each day—with eagerness at the prospect of studying math or French or literature. Rather, most students pause at the classroom door with a sense of uncertainty about how they will be regarded in the classroom. The need for a place to be known, appreciated, and cultivated as a person trumps the need to learn history or science or art for most learners.

Learning Environments that are Safe, Affirming, and Challenging

If the classroom is to provide an environment conducive to learning, for most students, the environment will need to clearly and consistently affirm that the student is accepted and acceptable as he or she is—but that the classroom will also extend the student's possibilities. The former happens when the classroom is safe and affirming. The latter happens when it provides a place for each student to make a worthy contribution to the community of learners, shows them purpose in learning, nets for them personal power through what they learn, and provides challenge as well as support for achieving the challenge (Tomlinson, 2003).

A teacher who leads in constructing a classroom environment that is positive for each learner communicates through words and actions a respect for each individual, a keen interest in knowing more about each person, a belief in the possibilities of every learner, a valuing of the uniqueness of each individual. Further, each student comes to see the classroom as a place that presents opportunities to "grow into oneself," and a place that supports development of each student's particular strengths (Tomlinson, 2003).

In such environments, it is clear to the student that the teacher works hard to ensure student success, is the student's partner in growth, is persistent in finding ways to make the classroom work for each learner, and spends considerable time reflecting on and planning for individuals and their needs (Tomlinson, 2003).

Learning Environments that Reflect Order and Shared Responsibility

Further, classroom environments that support success for a range of learners are orderly and efficient. They are not random, chaotic, or arbitrary. In fact, one of the paradoxes of teaching is that order is a prerequisite for freedom. Certainly order is necessary for the kind of student-centered flexibility that is necessary to meet the needs of diverse learners.

Classrooms environments also become stronger and more positive for a learner when that student feels a sense of shared ownership for the success of the classroom. In other words, teachers enlist the insights and abilities of students in developing, implementing, and assessing the effectiveness of classroom rules and routines (Tomlinson, 2003). Further, when students work together as a team whose members respect the needs and roles of each member on the team in promoting the success of both the team an individual "players" on the team, the classroom environment also offers students a positive sense of peer affiliation—another hallmark of a positive learning environment.

In the system that we call a classroom, environment impacts learners. In other words, where we teach will affect outcomes for who we teach. It's easier for a student to invest in success in a classroom where:

- that student feels known and appreciated by teacher and peers, people have time for that student,

- that student's language, culture, and perspectives are respected and included in teaching and learning,

- students' deficits are viewed as a normal part of learning for everyone rather than stigmas carried by a few,

- students' strengths are acknowledged, drawn upon in ways that benefit the class, and celebrated as valuable,

- that student feels success is likely to result from hard work,

- that student's need for adult and peer support is regularly addressed,

- that student has a voice and role in his/her own success and that of the class.

In many ways, the concept of learning environment is abstract. It becomes very real as we play out the roles of the teacher. How we greet students, talk with students, use time and space, establish classroom governance, implement teaching/learning routines, provide feedback, grade, and so on, ultimately communicate to students "how this place will be for them." Consciously or unconsciously we create a sort of classroom "weather" that will invigorate and nurture individuals as learners—or inhibit learner success. It is to our advantage as teachers and to the advantage of our students if we are conscious of how to build positive learning environments and realize the impact of each of our actions and decisions on the environment in which we teach and in which our students learn.

Understanding What We Teach

"What" we teach refers to curriculum. "Differentiation" refers to instruction. It would seem that the two are somewhat separate and could be considered independently of one another. However, in the classroom system where all elements are interdependent, the nature of curriculum is a critical determinant of student learning in general and of differentiation in particular.

To serve students well—and certainly to serve academically diverse students well—curriculum should be important, focused, engaging, and challenging (Tomlinson, 2003).

Curriculum that is Important and Focused

Curriculum is the chief vehicle through which we commend to students the value of learning. If what we teach is flat, rote, and disconnected from students' interests and lives, it's unlikely we'll enlist them as avid learners. It matters, then, that we teach what is most important in the disciplines and that what we teach seems important to students. In other words, what we teach should represent what experts in the various disciplines value, build student understanding of critical ideas and issues, and lead students toward expertise (Tomlinson, 2003). Ensuring that we teach what is most important in a discipline conveys the message to students that we believe they are worthy of learning and capable of mastering important things.

To that end, it is important for us as teachers to be able to specify the most important knowledge, understanding, and skill in each unit of study. Simply covering an acreage of information is not likely to result in retention, application, transfer or appreciation of knowledge for most students. Ensuring student understanding of what we teach is of particular importance. It is understanding (rather than memorization or application of skills out of context) that makes learning durable and useful. Further, the understandings or big ideas of a topic or discipline are vehicles through which we are most readily able to show students how what we teach connects with their own lives (Tomlinson & McTighe, In Press).

Clarity about the essential knowledge, understanding, and skill in a topic or unit of study is also essential for effective differentiation. Differentiation that promotes maximum student success will virtually never be quantitative. That is, it's ineffective to differentiate instruction for struggling learners by giving them less of what they don't understand. Nor is it meaningful to give advanced learners more of what they can already do. For both groups, differentiation should focus on the essential knowledge, understanding, and skill of a unit or topic.

Struggling learners need assistance in becoming proficient with what matters most in an area (Hopfenberg & Levin, 1993). Advanced learners need opportunity to expand their understanding of and ability to use what matters most. In both instances, teachers need clarity about what is essential to the discipline versus what is more tangential.

Curriculum that is Engaging

Likewise, we commend learning as a dynamic and fulfilling pursuit if what we teach engages student curiosity and interest. To that end, our curriculum needs to be intriguing to students, to help them see themselves and their world in what they learn, and to help them realize the value of what they are learning in their own lives and the lives of others (Tomlinson, 2003). What will engage one student may not engage another. Therefore, in a differentiated classroom, a teacher looks for multiple ways to connect the curriculum with learners—to engage their curiosity, energy, and persistence.

Curriculum that is Challenging and Supported

If the learning environment is to be positive and if students are to succeed to the greatest degree possible, each learner needs to see what they learn as both challenging and supported. When curriculum is challenging for a student, that student understands that his or her best is required to meet the conditions for success. The student feels extended or stretched. There is a "no excuses approach" to learning and students know that growth is a non-negotiable. Time in the classroom is "tight"—meaning that the teacher and students are consistently focused on important work.

At the same time, students consistently have a sense that there is ready support for their success. They are clear about criteria for success and about classroom rules and operational routines. They know there will be opportunities to ask questions, work with peers to master ideas and skills, and have small group time with the teacher for clarification and extension of what they are learning. There will be model work to guide them, organizers to help with gathering data and synthesizing ideas, different ways of taking in information and expressing learning, and so on.

It is the balance of demand and support that makes a classroom invigorating for learners. Each student needs the sense that there is work to do that seems a bit out of reach—and that if he or she gives a best effort to extending their reach, others will be "coaching" them for success as well.

Excellent teachers continue to hone what they teach over the course of a career. Developing and teaching quality curriculum is complex. It is also a prime responsibility of teachers. Differentiation must always be an extension of quality curriculum for each learner—and never a replacement for quality curriculum. Differentiating curriculum that is trivial, ambiguous, or boring will only generate multiple ways to an undesirable end.

Understanding How We Teach

A fundamental goal of differentiated teaching is ensuring maximum growth and success for each learner. Teaching with that goal in mind certainly affects *how* we teach. In a non-differentiated classroom, there is at least a tacit assumption that learner variance (a) doesn't matter, or (b) is an impediment to students' achieving desired outcomes with a positive attitude. In a differentiated classroom, the assumptions are different. Teachers assume learner variance is not only normal, but also potentially enriching in learning. The teacher's goal is to develop multiple routes for teaching and learning in order to maximize the likelihood that each student can find a "best way" to succeed with established goals—and even move beyond them.

"How" we teach is really the focus of differentiation, but how we teach is highly dependent on our knowledge of who we teach, our capacity to develop a learning environment that works positively for each student (where we teach), and our ability to design powerful curriculum (what we teach). It is unlikely that we can effectively address the needs of students we don't know and value. It's unlikely that we can attend to the needs of diverse learners in a classroom environment that works only for a few of them. And it is inefficient and ineffective to differentiate curriculum that fails to elicit student engagement and understanding.

While no teacher ever achieves a sort of sustained Nirvana in which the who, where, what, and how are absolutely ideal, we are more effective and professional when we work toward quality in each of these aspects of classroom practice and understand their interconnectedness. Certainly our students' success benefits from such continued efforts.

Specific strategies for how teachers might teach in a differentiated classroom will follow in the Applications section of this book. There are some key principles of differentiation, however, that form the basis for decision-making in a differentiated classroom. Briefly examining those principles is helpful in establishing a foundation for the practice-oriented section that comes next.

Key Principles Guiding Effective Differentiation

Principles related to any area offer us insight about how things work in that area. The same thing is true for principles that guide effective differentiation. They exist not in an arbitrary way, but because they are reflective of effective practice and help us understand how and why those practices work. The following are ten such principles and brief explanations of their importance in effectively differentiated classrooms.

    1) The teacher is clear about what matters in subject matter.

Having clarity about what is essential for students to know, understand, and do provides a compass for curriculum that both engages students and promotes understanding in students. It also ensures the ability of the teacher to develop work that is squarely focused on what matters most. In addition, such clarity provides a basis for extending the work of students who are advanced and scaffolding the work of students who struggle.

2) **The teacher understands, appreciates, and builds upon student differences.**

This is necessary for creating a positive learning environment for academically diverse learners. It is also a prerequisite for modifying curriculum and instruction in response to unique learner needs.

3) **Assessment and instruction are inseparable.**

Pre-assessment as a year and as a unit begins informs the teacher of student status relative to upcoming learning goals, student interests, and students' preferred ways of learning. Using pre-assessment data, the teacher can begin to make plans that address varied learner needs. On-going assessment throughout a unit continues to sharpen the teacher's sense of what is working and what is not yet working for the full range of students in the classroom. Ongoing or formative assessment data enables a teacher to continue working with students in ways that target their particular strengths and needs in light of important learning goals. Summative assessment should be designed to maximize student opportunity to demonstrate what they have come to know, understand and be able to do as the result of a segment of study. Summative assessment data can also "feed forward" into a next segment or unit of study so that the teacher is continuously gathering data on student growth and refining instructional plans based on the data.

4) **The teacher modifies content, process, and products in response to student readiness, interest, and learning profile.**

Content refers to what students will learn and how they will gain access to that knowledge, understanding and skill. Typically in a differentiated classroom, emphasis is on varying access to information, not varying the outcomes themselves. There are exceptions to that—for example, when students work with Individual Educational Plans, are highly advanced, or are new to the English language. It is also sometimes the case that a teacher "adds to" content goals by "working backwards" with students who have background gaps or students who are ahead in particular areas. Process refers to student activities or opportunities to make sense of and "own" essential knowledge understanding, and skill. Products refer to ways students will demonstrate their ability to use, transfer, and extend what they have come to know, understand, and be able to do as a result of a segment of study. By providing key opportunities for students to work with content, sense-making activities, and products in ways that are responsive to their readiness needs, interests, and best modes of learning, teachers provide maximum opportunity for success for each learner.

It is *not* the goal of a teacher to differentiate everything all the time, but rather to find key opportunities to meet learners where they are in order to propel them forward in knowledge, understanding, and skill.

5)   All students participate in respectful work.

For students to hold themselves, one another, and the work they do in high regard, it is necessary for the teacher to hold each of them in high regard. Among other things, that means each student should work with equally important, equally engaging, and equally appealing tasks. All students should work at high levels of thinking and with tasks that focus on essential understandings in a discipline.

6)   Students and teachers are collaborators in learning.

Students need guidance in becoming self-guided learners. In addition, classrooms are more effective and inviting when responsibility for their operation is shared by all members of the learning community. Not only does the teacher benefit from student insight on "how to make things work," but student ownership in learning is enhanced when their voices in the learning process are strong. In addition, students often have a clearer sense of what is working and not working for them than does the teacher who has responsibility for many students.

7)   The teacher balances attention to individuals and to the class as a whole.

An effectively differentiated classroom is a community of learners in the richest sense of the word. The students and teacher work for the betterment of each individual and for the strength of the class as a whole. In exactly the same way that an effective parent balances attention to each family member with the needs of the family as a unit, so the teacher seeks to make decisions and provide opportunities that build a sense of community and team while also attending to the unique needs and contributions of individuals who make up the community or team.

8) Flexibility is the hallmark of a differentiated classroom.

A teacher in a differentiated classroom is continually looking for effective ways to modify classroom elements—time, space, groupings, materials, modes of presentation, modes of investigation, resources, instructional strategies, and so on—to make learning as effective as possible for the greatest number of students. It is this quest for flexibility that is at the heart of differentiation. It is a representation of teacher creativity in search of solutions to the dilemmas and problems inherent in teaching complex content to a variety of young people.

9) Differentiation must always be "a way up," never "a way out."

Effective differentiation extends the capacities of learners. It never provides excuses or easy ways out. It always functions with the premise that a student can do remarkable things with appropriate guidance and support.

10) Goals of a differentiated classroom are maximum individual growth and success.

Rather than a norm-based focus, an effectively differentiated classroom adopts a dual focus on essential outcomes and maximum individual progress toward and beyond those outcomes. Rather than promoting competition among students, such classrooms promote competition against oneself. Individuals are likely to grow more consistently and persistently when they continue to challenge themselves to become stronger and more proficient today than they were yesterday. Reporting of grades, then, includes three separate measures: degree of proficiency with key goals, habits of work and mind in moving toward those goals, and personal growth (O'Connor, 2002; Tomlinson & McTighe, In Press).

Understanding the nature and intent of these principles is broadly useful to teachers in making instructional decisions that lead toward responsive teaching. Decisions that reflect the intent of the principles are likely to result in a classroom that works well for diverse learners, for the class as a unit, and for the professional educator.

Removing Barriers to Effective Differentiation

Research suggests that there are at least four key barriers to effective differentiation (Callahan, et al., 2003). They are evident in the practice of many teachers. However, since teachers, like students, are a diverse lot, different teachers experience different barriers to responsive instruction and different degrees of struggle with particular barriers.

For teachers who want to develop classrooms responsive to the learning needs of their students, it's important to be aware of the potential barriers to differentiation. It's even more important to ask questions in our practice that help eliminate or minimize the barriers. Following are the four common barriers to effective differentiation and questions we might ask to help avoid the barriers.

Failure to Reflect on Individual Students

Because teachers have to deal with so many students, it's easy to begin to think of "the students" as though they were essentially one person. We say, "The students liked the activity," when it's highly likely that some did and some didn't. We say, "The students just don't understand this," when it's predictable that some understood it quite well, some marginally understood, and some were lost. As long as we think about students as a "clump" rather than as individuals, we tend to teach them as though they were basically alike—which is seldom the case. To avoid that pitfall, it is helpful to ask ourselves the following questions and to seek answers to them.

- What do I know about my students as individuals?
- How well do they read? Write?
- How well do they understand when they listen?
- What's hardest for them in school?
- What's most engaging for them in school?
- How do they feel about their peers?
- How do their peers regard them?
- How does their culture affect their learning?
- How does gender affect them?

- What gaps do they have in their knowledge?

- What do they already know that I'm planning to teach?

- What are their interests?

- What are their dreams?

- How do they work best?

- What kind of adult support do they have outside of school?

- What kind of adult support do they need in class?

- What experiences do they have that can allow them to relate to what we study?

- What attitudes do they have about learning and themselves as learners?

Lack of Clarity about Curriculum

As noted earlier, clarity about essential knowledge, understanding, and skill is a precursor to focused teaching in general and to effective differentiation in particular. While the vast majority of teachers know what they "plan to cover" in a unit, many cannot designate the non-negotiable knowledge, understanding, and skill that shapes the unit and the discipline. Lacking that, teachers leave students to make sense of and connect with curriculum that seems disjointed and often purposeless to students. Also, without this clarity, teachers have no sound foundation upon which to differentiate instruction. Therefore, they either feel they cannot differentiate instruction because their job is to cover everything with everyone—or they differentiate by giving some students more work and some less, regardless of the appropriateness of the work for the student. To avoid "curriculum fog," it is helpful to ask and pursue answers to questions such as the following:

- What is this topic really about?

- Why does it matter?

- How is it organized to make sense?

- What would experts say is the essence of the topic?

- How might the topic connect to students' lives and experiences?

- How can the topic help students make sense of their lives and the world around them?

- What questions are essential to ask and answer about the topic?

- What are the key concepts that give the topic meaning?

- What principles explain the concepts?

- What skills do experts in the area regard as essential?

- How do experts use the key ideas and skills?

- What kinds of problems do experts attempt to solve?

- What in the topic can engage the minds of students?

- How can I guide the thought and work of my students to be more like that of experts in the discipline?

- What must students know, understand, and be able to do as a result of this unit of study and of each step in the unit?

- How can I be sure each lesson, task, and assessment focuses squarely on the essential knowledge, understanding, and skills?

Inadequate Repertoire of Instructional Approaches

We have good evidence that using a variety of appropriate instructional approaches in a classroom can positively impact student achievement, attitude, and behavior (Stronge, 2002). Nonetheless, many of us as teachers tend to adopt and use only a limited number of instructional approaches. Instructional strategies such as Complex Instruction, learning contracts, tiering, RAFTs, centers, WebQuests and Web Inquiry, and so on accomplish two potentially important things. First, they focus learning on the student rather than assuming that teacher-talk will result in learning. Second, they provide teachers with an opportunity to modify assignments to address learner need. If the strategies we use are limited to lecture, whole-class discussion, and completing worksheets, it's difficult to figure out how we might reach out to students in different ways. When we are comfortable with a range of effective instructional approaches, it is far easier to see how we can have learners work in various ways, while still focusing on essential outcomes. To avoid becoming too comfortable with just a few instructional approaches, it's useful to ask and pursue answers to questions such as the following

- What options do I have when I present ideas to students?

- What options do I have when I craft tasks and assessments for students?

- Once I have determined essential parameters for an assignment, what choices might I still give my students?

- In what ways might I honor students' varied learning preferences in presentations, tasks, and assessments?

- In what ways might I honor students' varied interests?

- In what ways might I ensure that students at various degrees of readiness continue to develop essential knowledge, understanding, and skill?

- How can I allow students to work in ways that are most productive for them?

- What modes of expression might I offer students?

- What modes of expression might I teach students?

- How can I support student proficiency with reading? Writing? Vocabulary?

- Which instructional strategies are good matches for the goals of the lesson?

- How do I know the degree of effectiveness of particular instructional approaches for particular students?

Inflexible Classroom Management

For many teachers, the idea of students working somewhat independently of the teacher is frightening—or at least out of the realm of possibility. For such teachers, "frontal control" is a way of life in the classroom. The teacher tells everyone what is important, gives everyone the same tasks and directions for starting and stopping tasks together, check work with the whole class, and so on. The teacher has the sense that if he or she is not "standing over" the students, then the students cannot and will not learn. A "frontal control" approach to classroom management denies students the opportunity to develop habits and skills of independent learners. It also perpetuates our inclination to see students as essentially alike and robs us of opportunity to address varied learner needs. To develop the teacher and student skills necessary for a flexible classroom, it is helpful to ask and seek answers to questions such as the following:

- How can I use time more flexibly?

- How can I find time to meet with individuals and small groups as well as with the whole class?

- How can I use classroom space more flexibly?

- How can I help students understand and appreciate their various strengths and needs?

- How can I make my students my partners in operating our classroom effectively?

- How can the students and I establish classroom routines that allow for responsible flexibility?

- How can the students and I practice the routines to ensure smooth classroom functioning when students work individually and in small groups?

- How can the students and I assess the effectiveness of classroom routines and modify them appropriately?

- How can I set up the classroom to allow both collaboration and individual work?

- How do I work with my students to establish and maintain appropriate levels of sound and movement in the classroom? How can I use materials more flexibly?

- What record keeping systems do I need to clarify goals and progress for my students and myself?

The Importance of Intent and Persistence

There is no single way to differentiate instruction—no one right way to reach out to students who need to learn in different ways. There is also no perfect classroom where everything is right for everyone all the time. What matters most in creating a differentiated classroom—one that can respond to learner needs often enough to make learning better for more students more of the time—is for a teacher to keep that goal persistently in the forefront of thinking and planning.

Taking first steps toward a definable goal is the way to begin any new and worthwhile endeavor—including a differentiated classroom. Learning from and along with your students can, over time, take you the distance you want to go in responding to each of the students for whom you share responsibility.

PART III: APPLICATIONS

EARLY STEPS IN DIFFERENTIATION

The Knowledge section provides you with some background information and principles to guide your thinking about differentiation. This section will provide concrete suggestions for beginning to teach in a responsive or differentiated way.

There is no formula for differentiation and teachers will begin responsive teaching in a variety of ways. The suggestions that follow are just that—suggestions. Feel free to substitute your own ideas about steps that will work best for you and your students.

As you begin to plan for and implement differentiation, consider two pieces of advice. First, continue to review the rationale for differentiation and the principles that guide effective differentiation. That should provide a compass for your plans and your reflection on how they are progressing in action. Second, start slowly. Few of us look like expert teachers during the earliest years of our careers. It's probably better to learn to do a few things comfortably than to try so much that you feel like things are out of your control. It's okay to move slowly in the directions you want to go. Just start and don't take your eye off the goals you have in mind—even if they seem distant in the beginning.

Following are some practical pointers to consider as you plan.

CURRICULUM FIRST, THEN PRE-ASSESSMENT

Work hard to articulate for yourself and your students precisely what they should know, understand, and be able to do as the result of a lesson, a group of lessons, and a unit of study. Develop the habit of asking yourself: (a) what in the unit will give students the most power to move forward with confidence in the subject area, (b) why the topic matters—what makes it worth learning, (c) why students should care about it, and (d) what you'd be embarrassed if they didn't know, didn't understand, and weren't able to do in a year or two after the unit ends. Emphasize those things—and take care of the others as you have time. Rote learning is fleeting (and dull). Understanding-based learning will endure (and will also make it easier for students to retain the less interesting details).

A worthwhile formula to remember is that "engagement plus understanding equals success." If we engage learners in what we teach, much of our job is done. If, in addition, we ensure genuine student understanding of what we teach, both our students and we are highly likely to be successful in the short and long term.

Once you can specify what students should know, understand, and be able to do as the result of a unit of study, you also know what should be on a pre-assessment that you give students prior to the beginning of a unit. (It's helpful to administer the pre-assessment a few days before the start of the unit so you have time to use in your plans what the pre-assessment shows you about student readiness.)

Pre-assessments don't have to be long. They serve the purpose of giving you an early snapshot of your students. You don't have to equate them with a work of art! Remember that pre-assessments should never be graded. They are simply to give you an early sense of where your students are in relation to the goals you have established as essential.

Even if you aren't sure quite how to use what you learn from pre-assessing early on, do it anyhow. It will remind you of the variety in your students and will be an impetus for your growth as a responsive teacher.

Practical Tips and Strategies	*Beginning of the Year Pre-assessments*

As the year begins, it's a good time to use some kinds of pre-assessments that you may not repeat—or at least won't use often—as the year goes on. Consider the following:

1. Get an early picture of your students' reading skills by giving them a brief passage to read and a couple of thought questions to answer in writing. Then, read them another brief passage and give them a couple of thought questions to answer in writing. The former will give you a sense of a student's visual comprehension and the latter of that student's auditory comprehension. If you have students who you discover cannot write the answers, repeat the assessment with the student(s) in an individual or small group setting and see if the student can answer the questions aloud. From this sort of basic reading survey, you'll get a rough sense of student readiness to read with comprehension, listen with comprehension, and write to convey meaning.
2. Get an early sense of what your students care about by giving them a brief interest inventory or checklist. You might list a variety of topics (related

and not related to your subject area) and ask students to number the five
they're most interested in and the five they're least interested in. Invite
them also to add topics to the list. Or, you might prefer having your
students write you an introductory letter, explaining what they like to do,
how they feel about school and the subject you'll be teaching them, and so
on.

3. Similarly, you might survey students early in the year to find out ways
they like to learn. You can again provide a checklist of options and invite
students to add information to the list—and perhaps to tell you a story or
anecdote about themselves as a learner that will help you understand them
better.

DEVELOP A MENTAL IMAGE OF YOUR CLASSROOM

See if you can make a mental movie of how you'd like your classroom to
look and how you'd like it to function. It's an exercise not unlike the one
Olympic athletes use leading up to important competitions. They learn
that if they can mentally see themselves executing a routine or maneuver,
they are more likely to accomplish the goals they have set for themselves.

Having a clear mental movie of what you envision for your classroom can
help you with room arrangement, thinking about classroom rules, planning
for daily instructions to students, and assessing how an activity, a class, or
a day worked for you and for your students.

Don't give up the images in the movie. Keep working toward enacting
them—one step at a time.

BECOME A STUDENT OF YOUR STUDENTS

From the earliest days of your teaching, make a few minutes every day to
study your students. You might watch them from the classroom window
as they get off the bus, or on the playground a noon, or in the halls. See
who has friends—and who does not. Look for leaders. Try to spot
discouragement or anger that's just below the surface in students.

In your own classroom, cultivate the habit of standing at the door each
time students come and go. Over the course of a year, you can have many
brief conversations with students—to let them know you recognize a new
haircut or that you were proud of how hard they worked with a difficult

problem the previous day in class or that you missed them when they were absent. Much of effective teaching is built upon teacher-student connections. Much of effective differentiation is as well.

In class, carry a clipboard as you walk around the room or lead a discussion. Make quick notes when you realize a student is having a particular problem with the work (or with peers). Jot it down when a student gives you a clear signal of an interest or of being very knowledgeable in a particular area. Note patterns of confusion or comprehension you observe during a lesson. You can file the notes in folders by student or class period. You'll be much more likely to teach responsively if you cultivate the habit of studying your students and the habit of reviewing your notes every week or so.

Also, have a time, place, or routine that invites students to share with you things that are working and not working for them in the classroom, suggestions they have for making the class work more effectively for them or for the group as a whole, or ideas for tasks and products in units you are teaching. Students often have insights that pass their teachers by— because teachers have to attend to so many details at once. Enlisting student insight can help the quality of instruction—and also gives students a sense of ownership in and responsibility for the success of the class.

PLAN FOR SUCCESS

It's easy to get so swamped in developing lesson plans that there's no time left to think about how you'll carry out the plans. In truth, instructional routines need at least as much time and thought as curriculum plans. If you have the most elegant plan in the world on paper but it invites chaos when you implement it, the elegance counts for little (at least on *that* day).

Go back to your mental movie. What would the class look like if it worked just the way you want it to? Run the movie in slow motion. How would you make sure students start working quickly when class begins? (For example, might you take attendance silently while the students are working rather than aloud as class starts? Might students turn in papers as they enter the room rather than passing them down rows while you and the other students wait?)

What directions will you need to give students? Rehearse them in several different ways. Which will be clearest to the students? Will it be more efficient and effective to give the directions orally or to put them on the board, overhead, or paper?

How do you expect students to work? Can they get up and move around? When is it okay for them to come to you or to get materials? How should they put away materials when the class or activity ends?

This advice may not seem like it has much to do with differentiation, and in a way, it doesn't. However, broad use of differentiation calls for a teacher who is comfortable "orchestrating" a classroom. That is, in a differentiated classroom the teacher sometimes has to direct an ensemble with multiple parts. Before we become comfortable with that sort of multi-directional classroom leadership, we first have to become comfortable with the elements of classroom leadership—giving directions, organizing movement, keeping track of student progress as they work independently, managing noise, starting and stopping activities, and so on.

The advice in this section relates to developing the "gross motor skills" of classroom management. Nearly always, they are a precursor to developing the fine motor skills of differentiation.

The trick is to become competent and confident in guiding successively more complex student behaviors. If you are skilled at giving the same set of directions to the whole class smoothly and clearly, you'll soon be ready to give two or three sets of directions for differentiated tasks. If you can get students in and out of groups in an organized way, it won't be long before you're comfortable having the groups work on different tasks. If you can have all of your students succeed in following directions at a learning center, you'll soon be able to have them follow different sets of directions or work with different materials there.

What matters most is that you inch your way toward a flexible, student-centered classroom—rather than allowing the classroom to become more teacher-centered and frontally controlled. Plan for success in small increments that allow you and your students to succeed in the classroom. That will move you progressively toward flexibility in guiding the work of your students.

TALK WITH YOUR STUDENTS ABOUT DIFFERENTIATION

At some point in your thinking about differentiation, it will be important to include your students in your thinking and planning. A differentiated classroom works better when everyone understands why things happen as they do. The conversations you have with your students will vary with their age and your level of comfort with differentiation. You might do something as simple as saying, "You seem to be interested in different kinds of books. How would you like it if the next book we read is one you select based on your interests and I'll figure out ways for us to have shared discussions even though we aren't all reading the same things?" Or you might say, "Based on your recent work in math, I think different ones of you need some practice with different skills. I think I'd like to try giving you homework tonight based on what your recent work suggests would be best for you. Then we'll talk about how that worked in a day or two."

Some teachers have their students graph their strengths and weaknesses within a subject or across several subjects. When students see the variance in the graphs, it provides an opportunity for the teacher to pose a question about how a classroom would work if it was going to be effective for each of the students when their strengths and needs are not all the same.

Over time, such conversations can enlist students in working on operational routines in the classroom, determining what "fair" might mean in a classroom where it's not always the goal to have everyone be treated exactly alike, and so on. As you and your students think through the ideas and issues together, you'll find you are more likely to have partners in the goal of creating a classroom that recognizes and attends to student differences.

THINK ABOUT "RANGES"

Differentiation is not a synonym for individualization. In a fully individualized classroom, a teacher would attempt a different lesson plan for each student. In a differentiated classroom, a teacher attempts to provide enough variety so that learning is a better fit for more students.

On one day, a teacher may assign one task to students who seem to be having difficulty with a particular idea or skill and another to students who do not seem to be having difficulty. Two tasks may be a "rough cut" compared to thirty-two tasks calibrated precisely to each student's exact needs. In truth, it would be a rare teacher who could so precisely define 32 different needs—and a rarer one who could manage to develop 32 tasks in response to those needs.

Thinking in terms of manageable ranges is necessary in large classrooms and can make quite a difference to students. So think in terms of ranges of options. It will help you and your students.

For example, a high school government teacher might ask students to explore ways in which the rights and privileges of the Constitution have grown to encompass more people and groups of people over time. The teacher might offer students the option of seeing how or whether a particular amendment has expanded to include women, African Americans, children, or new immigrants. That range of four options may not be a perfect match for everyone's interests, but having four options is likely to engage more students than if there were no options at all.

Similarly, in thinking about learning profile options, select some areas you feel comfortable in addressing and give students choices in those areas. For instance, you may ask them if they'd rather work alone or with a partner, if they prefer work that is more open-ended or more structured, whether they work better with movement and some noise or when they are still and when the area around them is quiet, and so on. You don't have to precisely address every need at every moment of the day in order to make a positive difference for many learners.

Likewise, as you learn more about the cultures of the students you teach, make room for students who learn best by seeing the big picture—as well as those who work well with parts of the whole. Make room for students who are reflective and reticent as well as those who are more overtly verbal. Make room for those who learn best deductively (by being told)— and those who learn best inductively (by discovering). Take into account students who rely on extrinsic motivation—and those whose motivation is intrinsic; those who prefer people to ideas—and those who prefer ideas to people. In other words, if you think about ranges of human preference and try to honor the ranges, you don't have to be an expert on many cultures to make your classroom a better fit for students from many cultures. Because there is great variability in learning preference within each culture, providing for ranges makes more sense than assuming that all students from a particular culture have the same learning preferences anyhow.

THINK INFORMATION, NOT GRADE BOOK

When you assign and review student work, develop the mindset that the work is most valuable for insights that it provides you about students and their needs. Don't assign work predominately for the sake of accumulating grades. After pre-assessing students and once your unit begins, every piece of work a student does provides you with useful information about where that student is along the learning journey you have planned. The work can help you see who is floundering and in regard to which key goals. It can help you be aware of students who need to move ahead. It can help you understand where your explanations or demonstrations have been clear and where they have not.

Grades for some of the work will go into your grade book of course, but that's not nearly as important to your teaching or to student learning as what you and your students can gain from viewing their work as a diagnosis of next steps needed for their growth.

In fact, it is a principle of best-practice grading that early work should often not be graded so that students have the opportunity to make and correct errors in an environment that feels safe. View on-going or formative student work predominately as data to inform your teaching and their learning.

OPTIONS FOR EARLY DIFFERENTIATION

You may already have in mind ways that you want to differentiate instruction for your students. If so, follow your instincts. If you're not quite sure where to begin, here are three options that tend to make a big difference in student success. You might want to consider implementing one or more of them in your classroom.

1) **Meet regularly with students in small groups.** If your schedule routinely included time for you to meet with subsets of students, you'd be able to teach ideas or skills in a new way for students who didn't grasp them initially, you'd be able to extend the work of learners who are advanced in a given area, you'd be able to help students who've been absent or read with students who need your assistance in that area. You can get much closer to student need when you can teach directly to particular needs than when you only teach to the class as a whole.

2) **Assign targeted homework.** Sometimes it makes sense to have everyone in the class complete the same homework. Sometimes, however, a particular task is far too difficult for some students and far too easy for others. In both cases, the homework becomes frustrating and useless. When your observations and assessment data indicates that some students are ready for more advanced work and/or that some students have learning gaps that need attention, consider occasional homework assignments that are targeted to such readiness needs. On other occasions, you might want to vary homework based on student interest or preferred mode of expression, for example.

3) Provide reading support for students who need it. If students are struggling with reading (whether because they are learning English, because they have a learning disability, or because they simply have not yet learned adequate reading skills), everything in school seems like an insurmountable problem. Think about your opportunity to support student reading in a variety of ways. You might encourage reading buddies or reading partners when students need to read text in class. You might model good reading with Read Alouds or Think Alouds in which you not only read key passages orally so that students hear effective reading, but unpack your thinking about the text as you go (in other words, think aloud about how the text is arranged why the author is using particular words or strategies, how you make sense of ideas, and so on). You might provide texts with essential passages highlighted so that students who struggle to read can work with key ideas in manageable amounts. You might provide materials (including text or internet sources) at varied reading levels. There are many things you can do to keep struggling readers from sinking and to improve their reading skills at the same time.

Practical Tips and Strategies	*Hints for Working with Small Groups of Students*

There are at least four guidelines to consider as you begin making small group instruction a part of your classroom routines.

1. Be sure students with whom you are *not* working in the small group know what to do and how to work while you are busy with other students. To

help students learn to work effectively without your direct supervision, you might want to teach everyone in the class how to work silently on a task according to particular directions and have them practice that several times before you begin meeting with small groups. After such independent work sessions, review with students the directions you gave them and have them assess their effectiveness in following the directions and completing their work. When you *do* begin with small group sessions, working independently and silently will be familiar to your students.

2. Use an "expert of the day" to handle student questions and needs while you work with small groups. You can designate one or more students as those who will go over directions, check work, help with skills, etc. while you are busy with a small group. Students should learn from the beginning that you are "off limits" (except in emergencies) while you are teaching small groups. All students can serve as experts in some way as the year progresses.

3. Use "anchor activities" for students who finish required work (or who get stuck and can't proceed) while you work with small groups. An anchor activity is a task or choice of tasks that a student automatically moves to when they finish work (or get stuck, until you are free to help them get un-stuck). Anchor activities should be purposeful and useful, but given the great number of things we'd like students to accomplish, there are many options for anchor activities that use a student's time to great advantage. Anchor activities can, of course, be targeted to a student's readiness, interest, or learning preference needs.

4. Be sure your groups are flexibly formed. Meet sometimes with students who have similar readiness needs, sometimes with students of similar interests, sometimes with random groups of students, sometimes with pairs of students and sometimes with groups of six or eight. Base your groupings on assessment data when appropriate. Be sure not to create predictable groups of bluebirds, buzzards, and wombats.

PART IV: EXTENSIONS

LEARNING AS YOU GO

There's at least as much for us to learn about the variety of students we teach and how we can serve them best, as there is to learn about the subjects we teach. Teaching remains exciting and challenging as long as teachers themselves are continual learners. The best teachers are continual students of their students as well as of their content. The resources below are just a few of the many available to educators to help us better understand who we teach, where we teach, what we teach, and how we teach—as well as the impact of each element on the others. Learn as you go and your perspective on your work will be new over and over again.

Books

Bransford, J., Brown, A., & Cocking, R. (Eds.). (2000). *How people learn: Brain, mind, experience, and school (Expanded edition).* Washington, DC: National Academy Press.

Cole, R. (1995). *Educating everybody's children: Diverse teaching strategies for diverse learners*: Alexandria, VA: Association for Supervision and Curriculum Development.

Cummings, C. (2000). *Winning strategies for classroom management.* Alexandria, VA: Association for Supervision and Curriculum Development.

Educational Research Service (2003). *What we know about culture and learning.* Arlington, VA: Author.

Ginsberg, M., & Wlodkowski, R. (2000). *Creating highly motivating classrooms for all students.* San Francisco: Jossey-Bass.

Gurian, M. (2001). *Boys and girls learn differently: A guide for teachers and parents*. San Francisco: Jossey-Bass.

Lasley, T., & Matczynski, T. (1997). *Strategies for teaching in a diverse society: Instructional models*.Belmont, CA: Wadsworth.

Levine, M. (2002). *A mind at a time*. New York: Simon & Schuster.

Marriott, D., & Kupperstein, J. (1997). *What are the other kids doing while you teach small groups?* Cypress: CA: Creative Teaching Press.

O'Connor, K. (2002). *How to grade for learning: Linking grades to standards*. Arlington Heights, IL: Skylight.

Stronge, J. (2002). *Qualities of effective teachers*. Alexandria, VA: Association for Supervision and Curriculum Development.

Tomlinson, C. (1999). *The differentiated classroom: Responding to the needs of all learners*. Alexandria, VA: Association for Supervision and Curriculum Development.

Tomlinson, C. (2001). *How to differentiate instruction in mixed-ability classrooms (2nd Edition)*. Alexandria, VA: Association for Supervision and Curriculum Development.

Tomlinson, C. (2003). *Fulfilling the promise of the differentiated*

classroom: Strategies and tools for responsive teaching.
Alexandria, VA: Association for Supervision and Curriculum
Development.

Tomlinson, C. & Eidson, C. (2003) *Differentiation in practice: A*

resource guide for differentiating curriculum Grades K-5.
Alexandria, VA: Association for Supervision and Curriculum
Development.

Tomlinson, C. & Eidson, C. (2003) *Differentiation in practice: A*

resource guide for differentiating curriculum Grades 5-9.
Alexandria, VA: Association for Supervision and Curriculum
Development.

Tomlinson, C., & McTighe, J. (In Press). *Understanding by Design and*

Differentiated Instruction: Two models for student success.
Alexandria, VA: Association for Supervision and Curriculum
Development.

Tomlinson, C. & Strickland, C. (2005) *Differentiation in practice: A*

resource guide for differentiating curriculum Grades 9-12.
Alexandria, VA: Association for Supervision and Curriculum
Development.

Winebrenner, S. (1992). *Teaching gifted kids in the regular classroom.*

Minneapolis, MN: Free Spirit Press.

Winebrenner, S. (1996). *Teaching kids with learning difficulties in the*

regular classroom. Minneapolis, MN: Free Spirit Press.

Articles

Brimijoin, K., Marquisse, E., & Tomlinson, C. (2003). Using data to differentiate instruction. *Educational Leadership, 60*(5), 70-73.

Nelson, G. (2001). Choosing content that's worth knowing. *Educational Leadership,* 59, (2),12-16.

Sternberg, R. (1997). What does it mean to be smart? *Educational Leadership, 54*(6), 20-24.

Tomlinson, C. (2002). Invitations to learn. *Educational Leadership, 60* (1), 6-10.

Tomlinson, C. (2003). Deciding to teach them all. *Educational Leadership, 61,* (2), 6-11.

Websites and Professional Associations

The organizations below have information useful in teaching students with various exceptionalities and/or differentiated instruction.

Council for Exceptional Children, www.cec.sped.org
1110 North Glebe Road, Suite 300,
Arlington, VA 22201
Telephone: (703) 620-3660
- The Council for Exceptional Children (CEC) is the largest international professional organization dedicated to improving educational outcomes for individuals with exceptionalities, students with disabilities, and/or the gifted.
  Their website offers a wide range of resources, even online classes.

National Association for Gifted Children, www.nagc.org
1707 L Street, N.W. - Suite 550
Washington, DC 20036
Telephone: (202) 785-4268
This is a non-profit organization that addresses the unique needs of children and youth with demonstrated gifts and talents as well as those

children who may be able to develop their talent potential with appropriate educational experiences.

Association for Supervision and Curriculum Development, www.ascd.org
1703 N. Beauregard St.
Alexandria, VA 22311-1714
Telephone: (800) 933-2723
- This organization helps provide a community of educators whose aim is to further teaching and learning for all students. It is a source for much information on differentiation including books, articles, videos, on-line courses, and audiotapes.

Teachers of English to Speakers of Other Languages, www.tesol.org
700 South Washington Street, Suite 200
Alexandria, Virginia 22314 USA
Telephone: (703) 836-0774 or (888) 547-3369
- A global education association, they provide resources important in the field of Second Language Learning.

International Reading Association, www.reading.org
- Their focus is worldwide literacy. This organization is an excellent resource as an educator.
800 Barksdale Rd.
PO Box 8139
Newark, DE 19714-8139
Telephone: (800) 336-7323

FOR REFLECTION

1. Think of a time when you or someone you know well was in a class that was far too difficult for them at the time (or a class that was far too easy). What was the impact of the class on the student in terms of attitude about the subject, attitude about their competence as a learner, attitude about the teacher, and even attitude about peers?

2. What do you suppose the long-term consequences are for students over time if they continue to work hard in school and meet with very little success?

3. What do you suppose the long-term consequences are for students over time if they continue to do very well in school without ever studying or working hard?

4. Mel Levine suggest that there are students walking the halls of every school who appear to themselves and others to be failures simply because the expectations of school about how people should learn are out of sync with the way those students learn. What are some ways in which you might adjust classroom routines and expectations to allow students to learn in ways that work best for them?

5. Lorna Earl, a Canadian educator, says that differentiation is making certain that the right students get the right task at the right time in order to learn best. She notes that once a teacher learns what a student already knows and what the student needs in order to continue learning, differentiation is not really an option for teachers, but rather an obvious response. If you could discuss that comment with her, what would you say to her? What would you ask her?

6. It's generally agreed that students are far more effective as learners when they are motivated to learn. In what ways to readiness, interest, and learning profile impact student motivation in the classroom?

7. Most experts in assessment and grading tell us that grading should flow from and reflect best practices in teaching. Many educators say that, instead, grading drives their teaching. In what way do you suppose beliefs about grading support or inhibit differentiation?

8. Discuss with a peer several ways you can accumulate insights about your students so that you can teach them more effectively.

9. When teachers are asked why they might differentiate instruction, most of the reasons they give have to do with benefits for students. When asked why they don't or might not differentiate instruction, most of the reasons they give have to do with challenges for the teacher. How would you want to balance those competing demands in your work as a teacher?

10. Develop a metaphor for a differentiated classroom that helps you envision its intent and nature more clearly. Share the metaphor with a peer and talk about other images or experiences that help you think about a responsive classroom.

GLOSSARY

Analytical, Practical, and Creative Intelligence   Three kinds of learning and expressive preference proposed by Yale psychologist Robert Sternberg. Analytical intelligence is "schoolhouse intelligence" and is most often reflected in classrooms. It includes preferences for things like comparing, contrasting, outlining, developing a well-supported argument, following directions, and so on. Practical intelligence is "street smarts" or a kind of application intelligence. It includes preferences for seeing how an idea is used by people in the real world and solving real-world problems with ideas and skills. Creative intelligence is "imaginative intelligence" and reflects a preference for supposing, looking at ideas in novel ways, changing elements in a context to see what happens, and so on. In a differentiated classroom, teachers can address students' intelligence preferences by using this well-researched model.

Expert Groups   An instructional strategy in which a teacher asks students to volunteer to become experts on a topic prior to the time the topic will be taught in a unit. Working with teacher-created guidelines, the students learn about the topic and assist the teacher with teaching it at the appropriate time in the unit. The strategy can be used in a differentiated classroom to extend existing student interests or develop new ones.

Formative Assessment   Assessment that takes place throughout a unit of study, after pre-assessment and prior to summative or final assessment. In a differentiated classroom, data from formative assessments helps teachers adapt instructional plans to address learner needs.

Jigsaw   An instructional strategy in which students work in two groups to complete a task. In the first group or their "home base group," they learn about the task, its parts, and their role in the task. They then move to a specialty group that studies one aspect of the whole task and prepares to teach students in the home groups what they have learned. Back in home groups, students take turns teaching what they have learned about the various parts of the task. In a differentiated classroom, a teacher can use Jigsaw to address student readiness, interest, and/or learning profile needs.

Problem-Based Learning   An instructional approach in which students begin with a fuzzy or ill-defined problem related to the topic they are studying. They make inferences about clues provided for them to identify the problem at hand, and they do research of various kinds to propose viable approaches to solving the problem. Most students benefit from well-designed and well-supported PBL tasks, but students with a preference for practical and creative approaches to learning may benefit especially.

RAFTs An instructional approach in which students are asked to take on a particular role (R), for a specified audience (A), and present ideas in a prescribed format (F), on a topic (T) that causes them to explore ideas central to the unit of study. RAFTs are very flexible and in a differentiated classroom can be designed to respond to student readiness, interest, and/or learning profile needs.

Read Alouds Any kind of reading done generally by a teacher in order to model effective reading for learners or to ensure that students have access to important material they might not be able to read on their own.

Simulation An instructional strategy in which students play a variety of roles reflective of real life roles in an attempt to understand a situation and topic. They learn important ideas and skills about the topic as they act out the roles and follow directions that are part of the simulation. While most students enjoy and benefit from simulations, students with a strong preference for moving about as they learn, for talking as they learn, for collaboration during learning, and for creative approaches to learning may especially benefit from simulations.

Summative Assessment Final or concluding assessment that comes at the end of an extended period of study to determine student proficiencies with key learning goals.

Think Alouds A reading strategy in which a teacher or a student who is proficient with reading reads a key passage of material aloud and simultaneously explains their thinking about what they are reading. The procedure is a way of modeling for students how a good reader interacts with text to make meaning of it.

Tiering An instructional approach in which all students work with the same key learning goals but at different "degrees of difficulty" so that each student is working at a level of challenge appropriate to his/her readiness needs. In a differentiated classroom, teachers can tier assignments, projects, learning centers, homework, and even assessments.

Web Inquiry An advanced form of WebQuests. Web Inquiry is an open-ended investigation process that promotes use of uninterpreted on-line data and information. Students learn to pose viable research questions, define procedures for exploring them, gather and investigate relevant data, analyze and manipulate the data, draw conclusions, and share findings. In a differentiated classroom, Web Inquiry is especially useful for students whose level of knowledge about a topic and degree of independence as a learner indicate that they have moved beyond the WebQuest format.

WebQuest An inquiry-based activity in which most or all of the information students use is drawn from the web. The teacher provides a framework and guidance for the inquiry to ensure that students are focused on using information rather than hunting for it and that they work at analysis, synthesis, and evaluation levels of thinking. WebQuests can be short term or long-term assignments.

REFERENCES

Bransford, J., Brown, A., & Cocking, R. (Eds.). (2000). *How people learn: Brain, mind, experience, and school (Expanded edition)*. Washington, DC: National Academy Press.

Callahan, C., Tomlinson, C., Moon, T., Brighton, C., & Hertberg, H. (2003). *Feasibility of high-end learning in the middle grades*. Charlottesville, VA: University of Virginia, National Research Center on the Gifted and Talented.

Gardner, H. (1993). *Multiple intelligences: The theory in practice*. New York: Basic Books.

Ginsberg, M., & Wlodkowski, R. (2000). *Creating highly motivating classrooms for all students*. San Francisco: Jossey-Bass.

Gurian, M. (2001). *Boys and girls learn differently: A guide for teachers and parents*. San Francisco: Jossey-Bass.

Hopfenberg, W., & Levin, H. (1993). *The accelerated schools resource guide*. San Francisco: Jossey-Bass.

Lasley, T., & Matczynski, T. (1997). *Strategies for teaching in a diverse society: Instructional models*. Belmont, CA: Wadsworth.

Levine, M. (2002). *A mind at a time*. New York: Simon & Schuster.

O'Connor, K. (2002). *How to grade for learning: Linking grades to standards*. Arlington Heights, IL: Skylight.

Sternberg, R. (1988). *The triarchic mind: A new theory of human intelligence*. New York: Cambridge University Press.

Stronge, J. (2002). *Qualities of effective teachers*. Alexandria, VA: Association for Supervision and Curriculum Development,

Tomlinson, C. (2003). *Fulfilling the promise of the differentiated classroom: Strategies and tools for responsive teaching*. Alexandria, VA: Association for Supervision and Curriculum Development.

Tomlinson, C., Brighton, C., Hertberg, H., Callahan, C., Moon, T., Brimijoin, K., Conover, L., & Reynolds, T. (2004). Differentiating instruction in response to student readiness, interest, and learning profile in academically diverse classrooms: A review of literature. *Journal for the Education of the Gifted, 27*, 119-145.

Tomlinson, C., & McTighe, J. (In Press). *Understanding by Design and Differentiated Instruction: Two models for student success*. Alexandria, VA: Association for Supervision and Curriculum Development.

Vygotsky, L. (1986). *Thought and language* (A. Kozulin, Trans. & Ed.). Cambridge, MA: Harvard University Press.

Wolfe, P. (2001). *Brain matters: Translating research into classroom practice*. Alexandria, VA: Association for Supervision and Curriculum Development.